# Passion Seeking Romance

# Passion Seeking Romance

## James M. Cunningham

iUniverse, Inc.
New York Lincoln Shanghai

# Passion Seeking Romance

iUniverse, Inc.

For information address:
iUniverse, Inc.
2021 Pine Lake Road, Suite 100
Lincoln, NE 68512
www.iuniverse.com

ISBN: 0-595-31515-1

Printed in the United States of America

To Paula R. Ridgeway
who taught me the true meaning of love,
and how to love again.

# Contents

# Contents

# Acknowledgements

To my parents, for teaching me that everything is possible through education.

—Jim and Mildred Cunningham

To a very special woman, romantic, writer, and poet that gave me early encouragement, and editorial assistance.

—Jade Walker

# Introduction

Sometimes, some rare and special times one meets a woman that can make a difference in your life. Over several years, I have come to know more about the woman that I am in love with.

The poems that appear in this book have been written to express the ups and downs of that relationship, and to ultimately express my opinion that love can overcome any obstacle placed in the way of happiness.

During one rare moment, I overheard her singing to doves while she was in her garden. I knew in that instant that she was the woman I had been looking for. Somehow everything made sense, and I realized that I wanted to spend the rest of my life with her.

After one year of dating I did propose, but she felt that we did not know each other well enough to make a lifetime commitment. For over three years now, I have worn the engagement ring on a gold chain next to my heart. The book of love requires that two people be on the same page, and turn it together. Some day, I would hope to find and experience love with passion, from a truly wonderful woman.

I have compiled this grouping of poetry to express personal feelings, and demonstrate love. All of these poems were written in letters sent to the woman I fell in love with. Over several years, we have become close friends, and will remain close friends for life even if she decides to accept my latest proposal. Since she so enjoyed the poetry, she has encouraged me to share the writings with every person that is going through the roller coaster ride of getting to know another. It was at that moment I decided to become a published author. It is my hope that a kindred spirit or soul mate may find my words to be what she is longing to hear from the man of her dreams.

Reflect upon this grouping of poems, as you may have found that man, and already lost him in your pursuit of the perfect man. I just want you to know that when a strong man falls in love sometimes, he will not come across the right way to a strong woman. Remember, it is never too late to change your mind, and go after him. After all, anything is possible in the pursuit of love.

The last poem in the collection is titled "The Question", and has been written for that special woman in this romantic mans heart.

# *First Kiss*

I am looking into your eyes;
Totally lost within their beauty.

Holding you next to me; feeling
The warmth and promise of your body.

For a brief moment in time; I sense,
Our two hearts beating as one.

The caress of your face, your arm, your hand;
Like the feeling of silk against my body.

The repeated touch of our lips; searching for the
Intimacy that only we can share.

The time to leave; a brush of mouths,
Like the whisper of wind against water.

I am left with the aroma of your perfume
And the passionate softness of your lips.

# Good Morning

The stark fingers of a tree limb touch the roof;
Keeping time to the rhythm of the wind.
Clouds race across the darkening sky;
As I snuggle closer to the warmth of the fire.
Looking at nature's wonder, content and dry;
My mind filled with you, my heart aflame with desire.

Alone and watching the approaching storm;
I see angry, crooked fingers of light shaking at the ground
I drift into sleep and dream all through the night.
The window captures a sprinkling of light from the rising sun;
And allows it to soft shoe across my face,
Alerting me, like the elbowed nudge of a woman.

Awake now, I listen to the raindrops spell out your name.
I lie unmoving thinking of your softness and warmth;
My heart is alight, and once again singing.
Am I still dreaming? Could you still be here?
The telephone rings; I lift it slowly to my ear.
Like a mild wind's touch, I hear in whispered tone;
"Good morning darling, I dreamed of you last night."

# *Choose Me*

Waiting by my side
Draped in golden mantle,
Dawn's caress awakens me.
Pouring from the cup of the sun
Sunbeams carry to earth stored up love
Allowing you to sip the liquid of my heart.

When we first met,
I was so happy to have found you.
I prayed to see love show in your eyes.
While angels stood in such awe of your beauty,
I petitioned the stars to dim in your presence;
Allowing the moon to be the highlight to your golden hair.

For unending days, I thirst with desire for you,
Tell me, out of all the men you have known;
Who did you love, that could be better than me?
Just cry out my name with biting desire,
The creatures of the night will hear you;
And carry your words back to me.

Unleash your passion to follow your heart,
Toss aside restraint and discard your dress.
Like a young fawn first entering a stream,
Plunge in naked, and feel the liquid of my love.
As I flow over you, forming droplets on your breast;
Choose me! Allow your love to quench this thirst.

# *True Love*

The pain you bear searches for relief,
My love attempts to embrace you;
I ask to hold your desires in the palm of my hands,
That I may provide a safe haven for all your dreams.

The secret you clasp tight to your breast,
Carries the weight craving you places upon my groin.
There is strength for you in being fragile once again,
Just trust your feelings, allow my love to heal the rest.

I have known you before time began,
And loved you throughout eternity;
My darling, for us there still remains time
On this earth for us to find each other.

First, you must allow the release of your heart
To combine with this now mortal heart,
So that we may allow our true love to......
Continue unabashed for another thousand years.

# Blue Eyes That Sparkle

Your eyes invite me to learn more of you,
I am curious—
You capture my attention with a single glance.
Now spellbound—
Everything around me continues on,
But my heart slows its beat.
In gentle voice—
You touch my memory with a tale of lost love.

Long soft hair cascades
Like a rolled bolt of silk unfolding
Upon the shoulders of this living statue
That does honor to beauty.
Caught up in the spell cast,
By the deep blue eyes that sparkle;
Diamonds form in the heart,
And are cut and polished by my passion.

# *Searching*

Most men search a lifetime,
Looking for rough stones in far off places;
Some they find in ancient riverbeds,
Others dredged from swift waters.
The earth holds its' coveted hoard deep within,
Now mined by sunken shaft; when—
If they just looked within your eyes,
Diamonds would gather in their souls.

I continue the search for the love
Of such a woman—
Someone to hold onto at night;
To caress, and share dreams with.
To make love, and listen
For the music, as our two hearts combine;
And in tender moments—
Find the soft rare beauty of her breast, my comfort.

# *My Rose*

The old man with gray hair is alone,
A small tattered bible held within his hands.
He stands above the open grave for a time,
Talking softly to the woman who now rests.

For over fifty years they were lovers,
Now he was facing life alone.
Their time together brought life meaning,
And still…she prepares the way for him.

All through the cold night,
The rain poured down.
No one noticed—
When he left the warmth of the house.

Friends searched for him, all that morning;
Only to find him, lying beside her grave.
His lifeless body, the nights' shelter—
For the woman…he would call…. My Rose.

# *Woman In My Dream*

The lovely woman marks her territory; just as
A lioness protects her hunting domain.
"Out……out of my space," she proclaims while
Gliding gracefully back and forth between tasks.

Setting a dazzling pace, opening drawers, rinsing pots;
Tossing greens, with such concentration and determination.
While juggling plates, place mats and settings; she lights candles.
All the while, carrying on a splendid conversation.

The artist is at work, and a wonder to behold.
She swirls and twirls; as I look on, a lock of gold hair
Falls gently across her face. Her magic is plied; and the—
Meal appears just in time, as the aroma creates such anticipation.

She proclaims, "I am not a formal woman." Yet, I know
In an instant that such a beauty would appear formal in any setting.
Wearing blue jeans in the garden by day; or
Evening gown at night attending a main feature.

I close my eyes and try to recall the woman of my dreams.
Why do I feel so comfortable? Why are you so familiar?
I slowly open my eyes, and there you are; I am actually sitting
Opposite such a lovely creature. And I now know—
I have finally found the woman in my dream.

# *The Measure of Love*

I bring you presents this beautiful day;
My love, and my heart as well.
With my heart for you; the sun and moon
And all that you can see of the wonders of nature.

From the mirrored reflection of distant stars;
Cast adrift across the vastness of the ocean.
To the timeless drift of endless sands;
Caught up in roaming the ancient deserts.

Just as stars at night and grains of sand,
Remain uncounted;
My love contains no way—
To be measured by mortal man.

Nor, can it be confined by boundaries,
It continues on forever...................

# *I Beseech Thee*

A book rested upon my chest as I drifted off to sleep.
I dreamed of love, of ancient Roman gods, and us.
I felt the pagan sensation of holding you close to me;
Entwined together like two vines pursuing the same tree.
The feeling of joy in the passion and tenderness of you.

I find myself standing before Venus, the goddess of love.
With a passionate plea, I ask her aid in pursuit of your love.
I request that she cloud the memory of this woman;
Clear away the hurt, and pain caused by lovers long past.
Provide her the will to take just one more chance.

Venus agrees to aid in this cause. I pray to the lovely goddess.
Do not fail me in your quest for I know you reign over love
And affairs of the heart are strictly your domain.
So take on this task; cure her heart, soften her resolve and
Reward my amorous advances.

# *Your Smile*

When I see your smile,
Lovely angels dance upon my heart;
Your beauty pours forth from within,
Filling full the caverns of my eyes.

While with you, I see only blue eyes,
They enchant, and coax me deep inside;
I feel your love, and see it turn to light,
As it enters and burns your image into my soul.

My thoughts are only of you,
You become the wind touching me;
The air all around that I feel,
For darling, you are the woman I love.

I long to hold and make love to you.
But how does one man capture the wind?
As you flow over the windmill of my heart
I breathe in the un-harnessed wind as you come.

# Love Flows Out

Darling, all I have to do
Is say your name, and—
You come to me in that
Special place within my heart.

You are the sun rising in my soul,
Creating the light for my love to find its way.
I can't get enough of being with you,
Even though you cause me to burn with desire.

Seeing you releases my love to flow
Like a raging river covering all before it,
A love that can take you places
That you have never been.

For now, the floodgates are open,
As my love reaches its crest;
You can watch it pass you and slowly recede,
Or take a chance and ride the surging current.

# *Release Your Love*

I awake at first light.
I turn to look beside me
To see if you lie there, still sleeping,
For my dreams of you are so real.

As I gaze longingly into your eyes,
The golden haze that is the substance of your soul;
Shows the hint of what awaits release,
The passion of your love, held deep within.

With an indefinable sigh,
You allow me to hold you close;
We lie clinging together, like vines
Climbing an ancient wall.
My tears touch then drop from your cheek.

The feeling of your warmth flows into my body,
Your heart beats like that of a frightened bird;
You shudder and tremble the length of your body,
As you melt into me, and release your love.

# Conquered

I look across the room and see you,
Your smile attracts me;
Laughter comes easy in your presence,
As you are the center of attention.

Men swarm around you,
For you have beauty told only in legend;
Your eyes search out mine,
They invite me to learn more of you.

You come to me, I am flattered,
Now I know your name;
You bring your lips close, and whisper,
"I want to be alone with you."

The hunger for love finds a place,
We kiss softly at first; then—
Passion takes over and I realize,
My heart has just been conquered.

# *Love You Forever*

Nothing built by man
  Can last forever.
Earthquakes shake, and
  Destroy whole cities.
Even islands that
  Are the creation of God;
Can sink beneath
  The onslaught of the sea.

Distant stars glow bright,
  Then one day dim;
Meteors hit atmosphere,
  And melt away.
Gravity holds everything
  In its proper place,
Except for the heart of this man
  In love with you.

A volcano lies dormant
  For a thousand years,
Erupts in an instant
  And sweeps away all that stands before it.
The hurricane reigns supremely at sea,
  Sinking ships it encounters.
Coming ashore
  It relinquishes dominion, and disappears.

Love reaches out to you…..
Elevating your mans hopes and desires.
While still holding onto his fragile heart,
Words spoken to you of his love

Have been dismissed by you as untrue.
Yet—if you only took the time to look,
You would see his soul shine with a love
That will last with you..........forever.

# *I Remember*

Seeing the path explored with
  The fresh eyes of youth—
I remember
  The special moments in my life.
Watching the glitter of fresh dew
  As it greets the day,
Or the last rays that linger;
  From a setting sun.
The first time—
  I could see the beauty within you,
I remember
  Fresh snow melting on a desert cactus;
Or the sight
  When light frames you in silhouette.

When I am close to the end of life,
  With my last breath,
I will recall the soft voice, and—
  Your words of love.
The sight of iris and jasmine,
  Within a manor garden,
The scent of your perfume
  When we embrace.
Your softness,
  As I feel the beat of heart against heart.
Cherry trees in the fullness of blossom
  By a cool stream.
For when I leave,
  My spirit will still find love with you.

# *The Sea As A Mistress*

The sea as a mistress,
Competes with the other woman
For the heart and soul of her man,
Knowing full well that she can only have one.

Both women are endowed with similar attributes,
For they can be—

> Soothing and gentle,
> Warm and comforting,
> Calm and nurturing.

Each can and will change in an instant,
Becoming—

> Menacing and rough,
> Cold and harsh,
> Angry and uncontrollable.

Both can be unpredictable,
Yet I know she is not a jealous concubine;
As her embrace allows me to return safe to land,
And find the comfort of my lover's arms.
For she knows deep within, that—
My heart will seek her out once again.

# *About You*

What is it about you
That controls my thoughts?
You are on my mind,
Both day and night
Even when I sleep;
You linger like morning mist in a dream.

What is it about you
That penetrates to my heart?
Could it be that I am in love with you?
There has to be some relief
From this constant burning desire;
Tell me that this malady has a cure.

What is it about you
That binds me to your soul?
Could it be that I seek heaven?
There has to be some way,
To end the continuous pain of loving;
Show me how the hunger can be fed.

What is it about you
That can make me cry tears of happiness?
Could it be that I have found passion?
If so, let me take you in my arms,
Hold you tight against my chest;
And provide both our hearts a place to rest.

# *My Love Was Here*

My love was here,
Before the Great Pyramids;
An ancient soul searching,
Throughout the known world.

My love was here,
When Troy was destroyed;
As Helen grieved for Paris,
I continued my quest for you.

My love was here,
When Egypt was conquered;
As Cleopatra wept for Caesar,
I went in search of you.

My love was here,
When great Rome fell pillaged;
The centuries have come and gone,
Yet, I still continued the search.

My love was here,
The first time I saw you;
Now time must stand still,
For I have found you at last.

# The Maze

I am lost chasing you,
In a maze of my own making;
To fall in love with you was easy,
Now I must convince you to love.

Each time I am with you,
My heart longs for your love;
At each turn of this winding path,
There stands the dead end of rejection.

Wanting you drives me to continue on,
I know this maze has an ending.
Just cry out that you love me, and—
I will find the pathway leading to you.

# *Loving You*

When I sit amongst the flowers,
They flush with color at my love;
When I hold an orchid, I hold you,
As I touch its petals, I caress you.

I walk beside a sacred lake,
I stop to take a drink, for I thirst for you;
Now prostrate, I glimpse your reflection,
As water meets my lips, I feel yours.

I see you everywhere in nature,
The dream of you resides inside the air;
Trees with vines entwined cry out your name,
Your love letters, the fallen leaves at my feet.

# *Fire Within*

I am afire
At the sight of you.
Just as smoke from an open hearth
Rises to the sky,
My heart is lifted aloft,
With the heat of passion;
The burning torch seeing you,
Ignites within my soul.

My heart soars above clear lakes,
And mountain tops;
Where only great bald eagles,
Dare court and mate.
They couple talon to talon,
And fall spinning to earth.
Come up and grab this heart,
Pierce it with sharp talon;
…and release the fire within.

# *Walking With You*

I remember the day you gave me,
A single long stemmed rose.
A gesture of love for a lonely man,
Walking the shore of life.

Its purpose served long ago,
It now has faded away, though—
The memory lingers, like—
A flat stone skipping across calm water.

I think of the precious lips
That brushed against my lips, and—
The tender hands that—
Touched my face that wonderful day.

My heart tells me that I should—
Never have let you leave that night,
For I would now sing; and—
Meet each day full of delight.

Still I walk along the beach of life alone,
Continuing on, my footprints grow fainter;
With each rising tide.
Each day the waves erase my passing, and—
Repair the bruised sand.
I now know that only your love,
Can atone for the damage to my heart.

Since our parting there is a void,
Within the depth of my soul.
Must I continue moving relentlessly
Towards the gray mist, alone?

Or be with you, filled—
With joy and happiness;
Walking together as man and wife.

# The Spark of Love

For one brief instant,
In that part of the universe;
Known as heaven,
I held the essence of you.
When our souls touched,
I know you felt the heat between us;
Weld our two bodies into one.

I sensed the restrained desire,
Within you beginning
To temper and liquefy your resolve.
Just as ice over a burning fire,
Turns to vapor—
Past memories of a love lost,
Can dampen rapture.

Open the way,
For my love to enter you.
Lower the barriers,
Placed to protect,
Allow me to fill the whole of you
With my passion, and—
Ignite the spark of love.

# Be My Love

Darling, be gentle with
 This old mans heart.
For it grows weary—
  Like the wings of a tired dove;
As it struggles helpless,
 Against a gale force wind.
Until at last it finds shelter,
 And can rest within your arms.

For now, the nectar of love
 Flows within my veins—
Its composition changed,
 Inside the chamber of the heart.
Chased onward by thought,
 Hot blood sent pulsing—
Like numerous lava flows,
 Channeled into narrow tubes.

I quiver along the length of my body
  When you question my love for you,
And feel the charred pain of love
 Passing through my heart.
Searing blood now turns to magma,
 Your words cooling the flow
As hot passion tumbles end over end,
 Into the cold sea of rejection.

I am left with the memory of you,
 And what might still become.
The image of the island
  We could have made together;

Had you only held in one place,
 The lava of my passion.
To become one with me—
 And be my love.

## *Love Hurts*

I miss your smile,
When you first see me.
I miss your laughter,
When I say something funny.
I miss talking with you,
About your hopes and dreams.
I miss your opinion,
On the important things.
I miss the encouragement,
That you freely give to me.
But............most of all,
I just miss being with you.

# *Over Time*

Having found your way
Into my heart,
Over time..............
Like a young tree
Growing against
A barbed wire fence;
You have become
A part of me.

# Small Happenings

Sometimes.....................
It's the small daily happenings
That make life spectacular.
Like walking in the rain......
Seeing you smile.............
Watching birds in flight.....
Hearing you sing to me.......
Finding a baby rabbit.........
Picking flowers...............
Or,
Just holding your hand.

# Sweet Anticipation

There is that moment
Just before I see you,
I don't know what
To call it, or……..
Just how to describe it;
But it's like taking a bite
Out of a delicious…….
Chocolate covered strawberry.
Two words that come close,
Sweet anticipation.

# *Desire*

An impish smile
As you gently toss
Your golden hair,
That special look
You have just for me;
You know….. the one
That captures my heart.

Sunshine finds eyes
That dance………
Like blue tinged clouds
On the wind.
Amorous, engaging glances
Provide a hint at the promise
Of great passion that awaits me.

Being in love with you
Allows my heart…….
The freedom to say
The words…..an ancient lover
Long ago whispered in your ear.
Come closer, desire drives me
To say them to you once again.

# Song In My Heart

Falling in love for the first time
Is being with you for just one moment.
The second my eyes catch sight of you
My heart becomes a white fluffy cloud.
You become its shadow below.........
Moving in response to my pure passion.

While I sleep my dreams are of you,
Awake I think only of you.........
Your hot breath welds me tight to you
Whenever I hold you in my arms.
When you kiss me...........
Love becomes the only song in my heart.

# *Apart*

When we are apart
My thoughts…..
Hold you close to me
Until,……….I can
Once again………..
Hold you in my arms
And feel the warmth
Of your body next to mine.

# *Love Struck*

I am going through life
Looking for a special woman.
Finding her, I will already know
She is the one I am in love with.

I know because every time I see you
My heart beats faster in anticipation
Of being together…..and, I behave
Like a love struck schoolboy.

I have been searching for you
All of my life….now, I must wait.
My heart tossed about like flotsam
On the tide, awaiting you to return my love.

## *Safe Harbor*

Take one special moment
Using your heart..........
To consider being with me.
Find the end to your journey,
Inside the safe harbor of my love.

Take one beautiful spring day
Using your heart............
To concentrate on loving me.
Watch the world as you know it,
Begin to change all around you.

Take the rest of your life, and
Give me your heart............
Discover what mine holds for you.
I ask you to walk with me for a time,
To embrace a love that will never end.

# Standing Alone

A silent distant Mesa sprouts from desert,
Layers of red clay veins stand exposed;
Shifting sands of an ancient ocean bed,
Display a barren, unforgiving land.

Sand sculptures are created by savage wind,
Mosaic art becomes forever encased in rock;
Vibrant colors splash about on a master's easel,
I see huge fir trees long ago turned to stone.

Shadows race across this sacred land,
The blue horizon turns to rose; as……..
It has for millions of years…I stand alone,
Realizing that my love for you is timeless.

# *Precious Time*

When a man lives his life alone
There is a part of him missing.
He can still have many dreams,
Mine is finding a woman
As wonderful as you............
I have already held you,
Every night in my dreams.
So seeing you for the first time,
Don't be alarmed that...........
I am already in love.
Until we are on the same page,
I will make each moment
Spent with you, a precious time.

# *Love In Song*

My heart lingers alone in the cold of the night,
Knowing that with you I will find warmth.
On the song made by a fast flowing brook,
My words of love are carried your way;
A ballad playing for all of nature to hear.

The stream fills its banks and will never go dry,
Not knowing the reason why it continues to rise.
I taste the moist softness of your lips.......and
Listen to the song you begin to sing to me,
Just as the love in my heart reaches its crest.

# *Distant Heaven*

I have come to know you now,
Somehow you have changed me.
Just to touch your silken hair,
To share the air you breathe;
It is the intoxication within
Each moment spent with you,
That takes me to a distant heaven.

# *Raging Flood*

Trickles of water that come together
On a mountainside....may find many
False fissures leading to the valley floor.
Yet, now a small stream begins to flow,
Carried on it...............
My love surges towards you;
At once becoming a raging flood
As it finds the correct channel,
That can deliver it straight to your heart.

# *In Heaven*

Do not speak
Of your love
Rather……..
Show it to me
With your smile.

When we are together
Allow your love
To come to me
In your laughter.

I find myself in the stars
Above you…..look up
You will find my lips
Gently nibbling on yours.

I have learned to love
You in two worlds….
On earth, inside my dreams;
Awake, I find myself in heaven.

# *Embrace Me*

Come to me
With.........
Open arms,
Take a chance
Once again;
You only risk
Losing your heart,
Once more
As we embrace.

# *Repeat In Song*

In all my life
I have never enjoyed
So much happiness.
In the quiet of the night,
I walk beneath a full moon;
Thinking of you......and
The memories we share,
I realize that I am in love.

Having made up my mind
That you are the one for me,
I resolve................
With every waking moment;
To pursue your heart.
Each evening, I even entreat Mockingbirds
To repeat in song my words of love,
While serenading underneath your bedroom window.

# Seek Your Love

I am not the most handsome man,
But you make me feel like I am.
I realize that with your great beauty,
You can have any man that you desire.

I come to you with an open heart,
To take a chance on loving you.
You make me feel important,
To make me want to love again.

I see you laughing once again,
You begin to trust a man again.
For several years you have been,
A companion............my friend.

Knowing the child and woman
In you, the way I do.............
It's no wonder my darling;
That I now seek more from you.

# *Forget-Me-Not*

When I think of you
I recall..........
Golden artic poppies
As the color of your hair.
When I am with you
I can see.........
Angelic chickweed flowers
Growing in the wilderness.
When you are in my arms,
I become lost..........
In the glacier filled lakes
That are your eyes.
When you kiss me,
I long to be.........
Your meadow of
Forget-Me-Not.

# *Leave Each Year*

When spring appears,
You come back to me.
All through the summer,
You hold onto, nurturing me.

When autumn comes,
You appear to change.
For a short time,
You cling tight to me.

When winter arrives,
You leave on the wind.
For you have become the leaf,
That now grows from me.

# I Walk Alone

Buildings of various pleasing colors,
Stand defiant against the ocean storm.
Twin church steeples seem to emulate,
Mountain peaks that appear in the distance.

Boat masts sway back and forth at anchor,
While angry waves make noise along the shore.
Gathered inside a weathered white picket fence,
Rows of stone crosses stand at attention.

Dark clouds race across the sky,
As cock weather vanes turn with the wind.
I walk a timeworn path alone thinking of you,
Drifting smoke appears as a stray lock of your hair.

# *To Dream Of Love*

Thinking of you on a spring day,
Half awake, I dream of love.
When our eyes meet for the first time,
You have a strange hold over me.
I am drawn towards you……..
Searching for the source of your power,
I attempt to scale the steep steps
Leading to your heart…but you continue
To climb higher, the closer I come to you.
I feel that I shall catch you in the clouds.

# Celestial Pathway

I look up at the stars
Searching for love.
Trusting that one
Will form……..
The celestial pathway
That will lead me
Directly to your heart.

# Risk The Heart

You stand in beauty
Above all others,
Like a lighthouse
Above a dangerous reef.
I see the warning beacon
Signaling to stay clear,
But I set a firm course
Directly towards jagged rocks.
I would rather run aground,
Risking the loss of my heart;
Than never to feel your love.

# *Sometimes*

Sometimes.........
Some rare and special times
One has the opportunity
To walk with a woman
For a time.........
And discover the difference
She can make in your life.
I am fortunate.......
For I have found such
A wonderful person in you.

# *Transparency Of Love*

I am a man
With feelings for you.
I create a canvas
On the cold window pane
With my warm breath.
I spell out your name,
Using my finger.
Placing my name under yours,
I enclose both.........
Inside a cupid's heart.
Now...........
When you pass my window,
You will discover for yourself;
The transparency of my love.

# Hollow Dream

If within the span
Of time..........
On this earth
We fail to find
Each other.......
Just the thought
Of not being with you,
Would make my life
A hollow dream.

# *Eclipse*

The sun appears black
In daylight...........
A dark void
That reflects a sadness.
My eyes fill with tears,
At the pain in my heart;
Because we are apart.
Then a crescent shaped
Light peaks through.....
I begin to feel the warmth
All around me, and......
I know that you
Will soon be in my arms.

# *Love Is Like A Butterfly*

My love is like a butterfly
With fragile wings lifting it aloft,
To be carried on carefree winds.
Floating flower to flower,
Looking for that special pollen;
Always landing with open wings,
I am easily dislodged by a soft breeze.
I find my rare flower at last, and
Taste of the nectar that you store
Deep within your heart.
Having found you….......
I realize that I can now close my wings,
Forever to the wind.

# *Allow Me*

When it rains outside,
Let us play in it together.
When there are storms with hail,
Allow me to be your shelter.

When the sun shines bright,
Let us pick flowers and wild berries.
When a cold wind blows,
Allow my body to be your warmth.

When everything is going great,
Let us share in the joys of life.
When life is rough and times are hard,
Allow my love to be the shield you carry.

# *Captured My Heart*

Like a beautiful melody
You play............
Over and over,
Inside my mind.........
I have been looking
Such a long time,
For a woman like you,
That the first time my eyes
Held yours...I knew instantly
That you were the one,
Destined to capture my heart.

# *Seeing You*

The peace I feel in nature,
Allows me to seek love again.
I listen to the song birds, as…
They sing of what's in my heart.

I am caught in a raging fire,
A burning love………
That just seeing you,
Becomes an all consuming flame.

The sun and moon will stand still,
Until the fire embers of my love
Develop into the stars that can never dim;
And……you are once more in my arms.

# *I Love You*

When I say, "I Love You" it must
Mean more than what others have said
To you so many times before.
The words are special when I say them to you,
Like watching butterflies dance on the wind.

When I say, "I Love You" it must
Mean that you are the only one for me.
I do not say the words without feeling them.
I want only the best of everything for you,
Like playing with dolphins as you swim.

When I say, "I Love You" it must
Mean that I want to spend my life with you.
A lifetime of doing things that make you happy.
How do you know that what I say is true?
Just listen to the birds as they greet you each day.

# *My Darling*

When our lips come together,
Your mouth opens like a flower.
The kiss is soft and long,
Bringing a blush to your cheek.

The soft crush of your body
Against mine.............
Allows me to feel your passion,
As you release a quiet moan.

My darling, having loved you in my dreams,
Everything about you is familiar to me;
Yet I still find you to be a mystery,
You must help me solve this riddle.

# *Love Song*

You have become
The love song
That I like to play.
A sweet……..
Soothing music
Repeating over and over
Inside my heart.
You continue to fill
My nights….and
My days……….
With your love.

# *Take My Breath*

Love.........
Suffocates me
With such
Intensity.......
I dare not breathe.
Loving you......
Permeates
Every part of me,
Taking..........
My breath away.

# My Heart Is Yours

My heart is yours for today,
The lake of love within just for you.
Swim in its warmth..........or
Rest awhile along its shore.

Be watchful as this lake is deep,
Although posted "No Trespassing"
You are invited to enter.........and
Discover what dwells in the depths.

You can enjoy for now the pleasures,
That comes from wading in the shallows.
I invite you to dive to the bottom,
Experience the beauty of my soul.

# *Perfection In Love*

Spend………..
One day and one night
With me, and
You shall possess
The source of all
That is poetry.
You will have
The best…of what
Night can offer,
Millions of stars
For you to see.
There will never be
More perfection in love,
Nor a greater place in heaven
Than there is waiting for you;
When the sun rises…and
Finds you content in my arms.

# *Away From You*

Each moment
Away.......
From you
......a day!
Each day
An
Eternity!

# Quiet Of The Night

In the distance
An owl calls into the night,
Nearby..............
Coyote howl at the moon.
Other animal sounds are heard
In the dense stillness.
I try to remember........
The way your hair looks,
To experience again....
The warmth of your lips
On mine.
I drift into.....and out of
A restless sleep.
My darling........
It's in the quiet of the night,
That I miss you the most.

## *Slow Dance*

I keep the image
Of you.........
Inside my heart.
It is there
That I hold you
Close to me.
I listen to the radio
Playing our song,
As we slow dance.

# Your Name

Just
To hear
The sound
Of it,
I say
Out loud
Your name,
Paula.......

# *Each Moment*

Gathering honey.
From an old hollow tree.
Picking wild blackberries,
On a summer day.
Walking in the evening,
Just after a rain.
Catching butterflies,
And setting them free.
Hearing your voice
As you say my name;
Brings the magic back
Into each moment.

# *One Day*

I am like
A young child
Eagerly waiting
To play……..
Looking forward
To that one day
You will say, Yes
And………….
Be with me forever.

# *Dreaming*

Am I dreaming
When you are
In my arms?
No………..
It just feels
Like I am,
Whenever I hold
You close to me.

# *My Thoughts*

When………..
My thoughts turn
To you,
Like the alluring
Fragrance
Of wild flowers
Cast upon……
A desert wind;
You……….
Come to me.

# My Love

Like…………..
Fresh footsteps
On a wind swept snow,
My love
Over time……..
Will find a way
To leave its imprint
Upon your soul.

# *If*

If you were
Snow falling…..
I would become
The mountain peak
For you to rest upon.
If you were
Rain falling…….
I would become
The basin
To hold you in.
If you were
The wind blowing…
I would become
A cloud……..and
Dance above the earth
With you.

# Gossamer

My love searches
For a place to dwell,
Like a silk string
Of gossamer floating
On the spring air.
Sometimes.........
When it lingers a while,
It clings to more
Than it can grasp.
In the attempt......
To hold on
It can perish,
When brushed away.

## *So Much Beauty*

After I felt
The sensation......
Of having a swarm of
Swallowtail butterflies
Touch my raised hand.
I never thought……..
In my wildest of dreams,
That so much beauty
Or such wondrous feelings
Would ever visit me again;
But then………you came
Into my life, and………
Touched my heart.

# Silk Wings

Wind, wind course over me,
Lift me gently
 Above the tall trees.
For I am like a butterfly
 With silk wings.
Brush up against me,
 Your sightless breath;
Carries me gently,
 To my beloved.

For my resolve,
 Swells the air all around,
Like a storm,
 Pushing the tide inward.
There are no barriers,
 Nor boundaries that surround;
Just the constancy of my love,
 Swept up within.

# *I Shall Call You*

I am in search of an endearing term.
An intimate name that will elicit instant recognition,
And seek out a response to words spoken with affection.
To call out that substitute name, and lovingly affirm;
That you know that I am the one speaking,

I shall call you, dearest!

Roses have been sent to secure your attention,
Providing you advance notice of my courting intentions.
Seeing the joy in your eyes filled me with such delight;
Kissing and holding you close has brought me into the light.
That you know that I am the one speaking,

I shall call you, sweetheart!

A strand of pearls from the depths of the ocean,
Have been placed with loving care upon your silken skin.
Brought to you out of love and made you smile once again;
To hear the sound of your laughter has provided me the notion.
That you know that I am the one speaking,

I shall call you, darling!

You are the north star at night, a bright light that is constant;
I know I can seek you out, and you will be there like the air.
I think of the garden where beautiful flowers abound, and—
The bee that gathers the queen's pollen, and turns it to nectar.
That you know I am the one speaking,

I shall call you, honey!

I, on the other hand,
Will respond to all of the above.
And, most favorably—
To three simple words;

Spoken in truth from your lips,
I love you!

# *First Snow*

The wind tosses about fragile flake,
Weaving a thick blanket for nature.
Trees gather white crystals
Within their limbs,
Then bow to the ground
To relieve the burden.
Roads and trails are hidden,
Lying beneath, layer upon layer
Of soft silk veil.
Once dark roof tops
Appear to blend, and—
Mingle with the clouds.

While on the ground,
Hiding under brush piles,
The rabbit hesitates;
Its heart beating fast.
Deep within,
The hollowed out tree,
The squirrel stays warm and safe.
For to venture out now
Holds hidden danger,
As the fox is on the prowl.

I look out from the window
At a blanket of snow,
Its fringe outlined,
By a warm water creek.
A thin mist rises to greet
Silent flakes falling.
Content—

I am warmed by the fire,
And thoughts of you.

# *My Love Is True*

It is that time of day, when turtle doves pair for the night;
Coo their affection and snuggle together to provide warmth
Against the chill of the night.
My attention is drawn to the flicker of a thousand miniature lights,
Floating adrift, rising out of and falling back into the evening mist.
While sitting and watching the firefly signal for a mate; I wonder,
How can I show you that my love is true?

You say no man can be trusted; and your heart still feels the hurt.
Night is here, and the blinking lights pair off; dim and fade away.
What can I say to show you that my love is true?
Should I change from perfect man to that of a lying cad?
Tell you only the words that you long to hear?
Would the lies cause the pain in your heart to clear?
I feel that I have done all that an honest man can do.

Dawn rushes toward us, as lovers embrace in a long kiss;
I watch the waxing moon reflect off your deep blue eyes.
I now know how to show you that my love is true,
And allow you to feel my words of love for you.
A temporary pause for now my heart can be hurt.
I am vulnerable, with my heart in my throat,
I ask you to marry me and become my wife.

# *Light Of Her Soul*

At first glance one could see,
Her love shining through blue eyes.
For me just to be near her,
Provides a sense of excitement;
The kind that comes from loving.

On this day we are choosing a ring,
With it to pledge our love for eternity.
A serious matter, we take our time,
For we are seeking the perfect symbol
To represent the love we both share.

A sapphire is what she wanted,
Set in the center of diamonds;
The ring itself, fashioned—
Like a butterfly in flight.
The luster within the blue stone,
Enhanced by the light of her soul.

# *My Love Continues To Grow*

The way you care about me,
The way you look at me,
The little things about you,

        Like singing to turtle doves.

The way your hair blows in the wind,
The way you smile at me,
The way your eyes sparkle,

        Only you can touch my soul.

The way you walk beside me,
The way you laugh with me,
The way you question life,

        Voicing your opinion.

The things you have done,
The places you have seen,
The loves that you shared,

        Each a part of you.

With each thought of you,
With every beat of my heart,
With each tender kiss,

        My love **continues to grow**.

# *Heart In The Clouds*

The clouds were passing overhead,
Images carried on a fast wind.
Broken and scattered they traveled,
Making soft white pictures just for me.

For one brief moment the scene above,
Takes the shape of a Cupid's heart.
I watch as it disappears into rolling vapor
And continue moving on.

Looking out towards the Northern Cross,
I watch the meteor shower approach me.
The drifting clouds block out the view;
Remembering that heart, I think of you.

Now, instead of watching the display,
I dream of holding and caressing you.
Enjoying the pleasure in that moment,
I am aroused with such a burning desire.

The wind carries to me the fragrance of iris,
A swamp exhalation of your vision appears.
I cry out the heartfelt words of love to you,
As my ardor probes for the interior of your heart.

# *Today I Fell In Love Again*

Today, I fell in love again,
As I saw your hair being tossed by the wind;
You remind me of feelings long subdued,
I have this stirring inside me beginning.
You continue to haunt the recess of my mind,
For the memory of you still holds desire,
While the hurting lingers close behind.

It is so easy to fall in love with you,
For you walk in the light of your beauty.
Yet, what do I now have to gain?
The lingering thought of losing you to another,
Would be more than my heart could stand.
I should know better than to open old wounds,
As my heart will again feel the pain.

Running away can be the easy way,
To avoid going through the pain of loving again.
No matter what I do, my thoughts are still of you.
Maybe if I take just one more chance,
And say the words of love I have for you;
I wonder....would you come to me this time?
For today, I fell in love again.

# *The Woman I Love*

The siren songs of love,
Carried on distant wind are calling,
Pulling us towards a tropical paradise,
Far out to sea.
Darling, it's there that we are heading,
To view white capped waves
As far as the eye can see.

Walking with you at night,
I watch the moon reflecting
Off your deep blue eyes, and—
Be the highlight to your golden hair.
The island is merely God's stage
For such a romantic setting;
For you to nurture new feelings, and—
Discover just how much I care.

# *You Are The One*

If I could just live my life
 As a perfect dream—
You would be the woman
 That stands beside me.
Whenever I dream of love,
 You are there;
As you whisper into my ear,
 My soul answers.

When our eyes meet
 I am held within that moment,
As if caught up in a silken web,
 Spread unseen, by a spider.
My heart struggles to break free,
 And becomes more entangled;
Now captured—helpless and afraid,
 It is yours to have.

A year passes by,
 And I am still dangling from silken thread;
Time no longer has a purpose,
 Only the moments spent with you.
I ask you to be mine, and—
 Release the silk wrappings around my heart;
You decline, the broken pieces now discarded,
 Drop to the ground.

Time now has a purpose,
 I decide to continue the pursuit;
It takes me several years,
 We had to become friends before lovers.

Even though my heart was aching—
 I had to see, and be near you;
Because, my darling,
 I have known from the very beginning
That you are the one!

# My Two Hearts

I think of you and—
 My emotions rise out of control from within.
A tear wells up in the corner of each eye
 And drops into the channels
Burrowed  from years of carrying the pain,
 And burden of a lost love.
For to try, or to trust again;
 The dry reservoir must refill to the brim.

Until this time, I avoided the—
Sensation of loving, and being loved again.
But now my broken heart has split apart;
 In place of one, I now have two.
One to provide love, comfort
 From pain, anger and the scars of rejection.
The other to pursue the fullness of love,
 And shower you with affection.

You are with me, moment to moment,
 Truly our love must have meaning.
My soul has been searching for a jewel,
 Only to find this hidden treasure.
Just to feel your touch,
 Is to experience the caress of fine lace.
To hear your voice, the sound—
 Travels to me, like a soft desert breeze.

There is no turning back for us now;
 I give my love to you freely.
Which ever path we choose,
 To love again is a risk worth taking.

For the joy, or the pain,
 That can come from loving you
Now has a special place to go
Within the chambers of my two hearts.

# *To Love Again*

Off the cutting room floor of our scarlet past,
Taken from fragments titled, "Young Lovers,"
Your image, once brilliant splices together.
Though now dulled from the passage of time,
In tinted color, you make your debut;
Your lips move and form yet unspoken words.

With my eyes tightly closed,
Searching the dusty alcoves of memory,
I endeavor to recall,
The youthful love affair.
Remembering intimate moments we shared,
A silent movie plays inside my mind.

As if dubbed, a part of the film,
Unwinds from the reel;
For to see you releases this dormant heart.
Now recalling the lost love of our youth,
Regretting the years spent without you;
I have come home to ask you to love again.

# Come Along With Me

The wide expanse of the sea
Beckons to me.
It tempts me
To seek the far off shores.
The stagnant solitude
Cries out
For a new companion.

I can hear the sound
Made by tall masts straining,
Feel the wood
Embrace the waves;
Cold spray breaking upon the deck.
A stout ship underway,
With full sail running ahead.

The siren songs,
Carried by the wind
 Whisper into my ear.
There are new places to see.
Yet now I have found love,
And must resist.
Unless, she would come along with me.

# *Thoughts Of You*

Let me unwrap you,
And hold you within
These tender arms
Which now have strength
For only you.

Provide my eyes,
The sight of you,
Naked, untouched
By imperfection.

Violate my senses,
Allow the fragrance of your
Body to permeate mine;
Bind our lips and thighs tight
With a rope made of jasmine.
Remain bound to me
Long after passion recedes.

# *I Miss You*

I miss you when I first awake
As first light starts my day.
I move close to you,
Until I feel the warmth of your body,
And see the beauty of your smile.

I miss you throughout the day.
Everywhere I turn,
It is barren and dark without you;
Until I see the hint of mischief in your eyes,
Or hear the laughter of the little girl within.

I miss you as day turns to night,
When daylight steals away.
I am totally lost unless you seek me out,
Until you tell me that I am the only one
Who can provide your heart shelter.

I know that you could choose,
To be with another…
Yet darling, I can love only you.
I sleep at your side, and still;
I miss you as I dream.

# *Loneliness*

Each morning, I awake alone.
I have become accustomed to the routine.
With breakfast there is no discussion,
Only a single place setting awaits me.
No one to say, "Have a nice day."
Every so often, I shed a tear—
For I feel lost, and no one knows to search.

During the day, there is no time to be social;
Beautiful women greet me with a smile.
My heart yells at me as they pass by.
Only the mind hears what my thoughts call out.
I struggle within myself, and try to talk,
They are gone, before I gain the courage to speak.
If only I wasn't so shy; I must try harder next time.

When I arrive home, no warm greeting awaits;
Instead the night embraces me with cold solitude.
Life has gone on this way for many years.
It takes time to find just the right companion.
There must be more to life, than living this way.
This time, there is no tomorrow—
Darkness continues to hold me to its bosom.

# *Worthy*

The last time you were in my arms,
Your eyes held the reflection of my love.
I felt the energy surge between us,
Yet you chose to remain aloof.

To offer one's love, and have it rejected;
Rips and tears at the heart of any man.
Yet, without your love, I can find no peace;
I endure the pain in solitude.

The sapphire ring I presented to you;
Is now carried by me on golden chain.
The cool blue stone touching my heart,
A symbol of my love; it is safe there.

We waste precious time; I must be careful
With what remains, for my heart carries the
Burden of passing years. Without you—
Days feel shorter, the nights seem longer.
Loneliness haunts and surrounds like a cold grave.

Watching the heavens through the night, I wonder,
Can each distant star hold the love in a mans heart?
It now becomes clear to me.
I must pursue your love, like a star chasing the dawn;
For you are my sunshine and worthy of the effort.

# Love Pours Out

When I see you, my heart
Pushes through my chest.
I am afraid to close my eyes,
For upon opening again; and—
Seeing you, my heart will surely burst.

I can not sleep at night,
Nor will I for some time.
There's a lot I do not understand
About this feeling I have; but—
I do know there is no way of changing it.

I brush aside all other thoughts,
Except those that come from loving you.
I must have you in my life, say yes—
Or you will view the image of a broken heart;
Just look upon me as my love pours out.

# Set Me Free

The feelings I have for you,
Come from deep within me.
They reside in a special place,
Reserved only for your love.

The chambers of my heart,
Are heated with burning desire,
Releasing hot passion to chase,
After thoughts of you.

Like the approaching fog
That hides all that it encounters,
This longing for you creates a haze,
That clouds over every thought
Except of my love for you.

Tell me how to find release from this misery.
Can this pain that comes
From loving you be soothed?
Or, should I now pursue another?
Darling, you must return my love,
Or set me free.

# *The Canyon Of Lost Dreams*

Just the thought of touching you
Sends my heart soaring;
Making it difficult for me to breathe,
In heights that are devoid of air.

I concentrate on being with you,
And like walking in the rain;
You come to me in droplets.
I feel your presence all around.

You are real; yet a dream,
A part of me found deep within.
Much like touching my shadow;
You are there, but I can't hold you.

My heart catches in an ancient chasm,
Floating on a fast river into the unknown.
For the course set by you has unseen waters;
Yet I am still attempting to love.

I look up at the night stars in search of intimacy;
Like you, they appear to be far above my grasp.
Reaching up to touch, they reject me.
And I continue to stay afloat;
Adrift in the canyon of lost dreams.

# *Remove the Thorn*

Loving you has provided my passion wings,
Allowing me to make love to you above the clouds.
Since we parted last, I continue to watch the sunset alone.
If I could command the night to stay in just one place,
I would have the moon reflect your beauty upon it,
So that I could see you from anywhere on earth.

If I could command all the seasons,
Every month would become like springtime.
Flowers blooming all year to compliment your beauty;
Their falling petals making up the bed for you to lie upon.
A warm breeze would carry my love only to you,
Across the wide distance that separates two lovers hearts.

In my haste to win your love, I leave the well-traveled path.
I fall head on into bramble and briar,
The thorns scratch and tear at my heart,
I become aware of your fragrance as you approach;
Attempting to free myself, I reach out to you.
First you must remove the thorn holding firm my heart.

# How Quietly

How quietly my love has slipped away,
Into that emptiness from whence it came.
The passing days turn to gray,
From ash lifted aloft from a now dormant volcano.
For me the red roses have lost their color,
While my dreams flee on a gust of drifting wind.
My love fades into the evening mist,
I am lonely; your love is surely what I miss.

Each setting sun marks the time remaining for me,
As light steals my days and moves me into darkness.
Flowers wilt, petals fall, as true love has gone astray.
I am left with thoughts of you, and memories we shared.
Now each sunset shows me just the color of gray,
How quietly my love has slipped away.

# Come To Me

As the dreams of our youth fade,
And the heart mourns their passing.
If time allows reprieve,
Happiness still awaits you.
Do not be timid, for time cheats lovers.
So darling, do not forget—
You can come to me, without condition,
And experience the joy of our love.

If, when one day you awake,
Nothing appears as you thought it to be.
When your beauty begins to fade, and—
The mirror reflects a portrait of loneliness,
Happiness can still be shared, if time allows.
So darling, do not forget—
You can come to me,
And your heart will find mine waiting.

# *To Paula*

I love you,

> because there are butterflies
>
> because there are song birds
>
> because there are flowers
>
> > that provide fragrance to the air.

I love you,

> because there are clear lakes
>
> because there are cool streams
>
> because there are rivers
>
> > that flow into the oceans.

I love you,

> because of your smile
>
> because of your beauty
>
> because of your heart
>
> > that shows the pureness of your soul.

I love you,

> because to do otherwise
>
> > would mean that I had never lived.

# *The Question*

The gold chain that I wear,
Holds the key to the question,
That only you
Can provide the answer.

These words all combine to complete a quest.
Knowing my heart can never rest
Until I hear from your lips,
The words that will resolve this mystery.

Darling, will your answer bring us together?
Or once said forever keep us apart?
Remove the golden chain found over my heart,
Place the ring, my pledge of love upon your hand,
I ask you with all my love to marry me, to be my wife.

# *Biography*

James Cunningham was born and raised in St. Louis, Mo. While receiving a Christian education, he studied Latin for fourteen years, and had the opportunity to study French from the Cambodia Royal Academy. He is a graduate of St. Louis University holding a Bachelor of Science Degree in Finance and Accounting. He completed additional course study at Stanford University.

Cunningham has worked as the senior executive of various financial institutions. He has traveled to Portugal, Spain Switzerland, England, Germany, Italy, France, Ireland, Scotland, Turkey, India, Thailand, Cambodia and Laos.

It was during his time spent in Europe and the Far East that the experiences, memories and the intense romantic feelings descriptive in a number of these poems had their origins.

It took the encouragement of one special woman to allow the words to find their way.

Cunningham lives in Texas and is currently working on his first novel.